GW01417538

DEVELOPING SCIENTIFIC ENQUIRY 6

ANNE BUNCE

**ANNE WHITEHEAD
(SERIES CONSULTANT)**

© 2001 Folens Limited, on behalf of the author.

United Kingdom: Folens Publishers, Apex Business Centre, Boscombe Road, Dunstable, LU5 4RL.
Email: folens@folens.com

Ireland: Folens Publishers, Greenhills Road, Tallaght, Dublin 24.
Email: info@folens.ie

Poland: JUKA, ul. Renesansowa 38, Warsaw 01-905.

Editor: Julia Boore
Layout artist: Suzanne Ward
Cover design: Martin Cross
Illustrations: Susan Hutchison (Graham-Cameron Illustration)
Cover photographs: Paul Franklin and GI Bernard (Oxford Scientific Films)

The author and publishers would like to thank all teachers, particularly RE, AJ, AP and LW, involved in putting together the 'fan diagram' on pages 6–7.

First published 2001 by Folens Limited.
Reprinted 2001.

British Library Cataloguing in Publication Data. A catalogue record for this book is available from the British Library.

ISBN 1 84163759-9

CONTENTS

Introduction 4

Progression in Scientific Enquiry 5

Lesson Plans 12

Interdependence and Adaptation 14

Micro-organisms 16

More About Dissolving: 1 18

More About Dissolving: 2 20

Reversible and Irreversible Changes 23

Forces in Action 24

How We See Things 26

Changing Circuits 28

Enquiry in Technological and Environmental Contexts: 1 30

Enquiry in Technological and Environmental Contexts: 2 32

Pupil Sheets 35

INTRODUCTION

This book provides additional support for users of any teaching scheme compatible with the Scheme of Work for Primary Science published by the Qualifications and Curriculum Authority (QCA) for England.

Developing Scientific Enquiry 6 is designed to help plan and assess Year 6 children's skills of scientific enquiry and to provide differentiated work to move them forward in their learning. The activities can be used as they are, or adapted to achieve differentiation in a wider range of investigative work.

The scientific story

Scientists try to explain how our world works and gather evidence to test ideas. They think creatively, develop explanations and then gather and examine evidence to test these ideas. Sometimes their views will be corroborated, but at other times there will be discrepancies between their ideas and their evidence. These discrepancies lead to another period of reflection and creative thought. In this way, knowledge and understanding of the world is refined, revised and developed. Children can develop their own understanding of the world by similar means. They cannot test everything, but they should come to appreciate that scientific ideas are based on the best available evidence.

Investigation

An investigation involves the children in raising questions that can be tested by gathering evidence and then scrutinising it to build scientific knowledge and understanding. There are many ways to find out the answer to a question. When asked open-ended questions, children are more likely to offer their own observations, questions, ideas and interpretations. One of the greatest skills in teaching scientific enquiry is that of listening to children's ideas and helping children to develop them further without imposing your own. Their ideas are not always scientifically correct – an incorrect prediction can be tested by the children, as long as the discussion draws out that the evidence does not support the prediction made.

This book contains:
◆ **Progression in scientific enquiry**
   This summarises the range of skills used in investigative work in Year 6 and details how these skills are manifested and encouraged at different levels of attainment. This section will enable you to assess the children's level of performance and identify teaching strategies that will help you move them on to the next level.

◆ **Lesson plans and pupil sheets**
   The plans show detailed examples of how a lesson or series of lessons can be used to develop specific enquiry skills at the different levels. The learning objectives correspond to those in the QCA Scheme of Work for Primary Science. The Numeracy cross-curricular links correspond directly with the National Numeracy Strategy. At the end of the book, there are photocopiable pupil sheets that can be matched to the children's ability.

PROGRESSION IN SCIENTIFIC ENQUIRY

The diagram on pages 6–7 shows how the children will proceed from an active starting point to initiate and plan an investigation, obtain and present relevant evidence, then consider evidence and evaluate work. Each area involved in scientific enquiry is shown. The diagram can be used:
- to plan how to support and extend children's knowledge at both ends of the ability range
- to plan which children are ready for more difficult tasks
- as criteria for assessment
- to track individual progress
- to set targets for individuals, groups and classes
- to serve as a record by colouring in relevant sections on a copy devoted to each child.

Any of the skills can be addressed and developed separately, or development may be focused on linked sets of skills. The different sections of the diagram are explained below.

Investigative work involves the children in formulating questions and ideas to be investigated. The inspiration may come from a range of sources (including your own questions), but it is important that the children think through what they are going to investigate and their purpose for doing so. Some starting points can be sources of first-hand information, including the results of previous investigations or other observations they have made. Others include the use of secondary sources such as books, CD-ROMs, computer programs, other children's work, posters, videos, tapes, educational visits, television programmes, newspapers and photographs.

The active starting point

Eliciting children's previous learning provides a stimulus for the starting point. There is a variety of techniques. For a topic on sound, for example, you could use:

Eliciting children's previous learning

Experience with phenomena	Play sound makers or go on a sound walk
Book browse	Look for animals with different ears
Interactive display	Display sound blockers/helpers (e.g. ear muffs, ear trumpet)
Diary	Record sounds heard during the day
Brainstorm	Brainstorm knowledge about sounds
Concept map	Elicit links between held ideas
Drawing	Annotate pictures of sound makers to show scientific ideas that the children hold
Collection	Collect sound makers of a variety of materials and sounds
Card sort	Sort sounds into those that are easy/difficult to hear
Games	Blindfold children in turn and ask them to point in the direction of sounds heard
Floor book	Formulate a list of questions arising from class discussion
Technology in action	Make a device to help people hear better
Cartoon	Use a cartoon of children discussing sound makers and which will be the easiest to hear. Discuss class ideas.

Exploring and reflecting involve direct engagement of the children with the information sources. In the early stages, this is play. Later exploration is more systematic, rigorous, focused and conscious. Through discussion, the children reflect on ideas and begin to draw on scientific skills. Exploration can be first-hand, or focused on secondary sources. For example, during a book browse, children could notice that some animals have disproportionately large ears for their size while others have no visible ears.

Exploring and reflecting

Observation and discussion encourages the children to respond to the starting point. Their initial reflection may lead them to carry out more focused observation. The discussions they have with their peers, adults or teacher can help them develop their own ideas and questions.

Observing and discussing

'Communicating' is shown on the diagrams as strengthening struts between the different sections. Throughout any enquiry, children should be communicating through oral and written work.

Communicating

OBTAINING AND

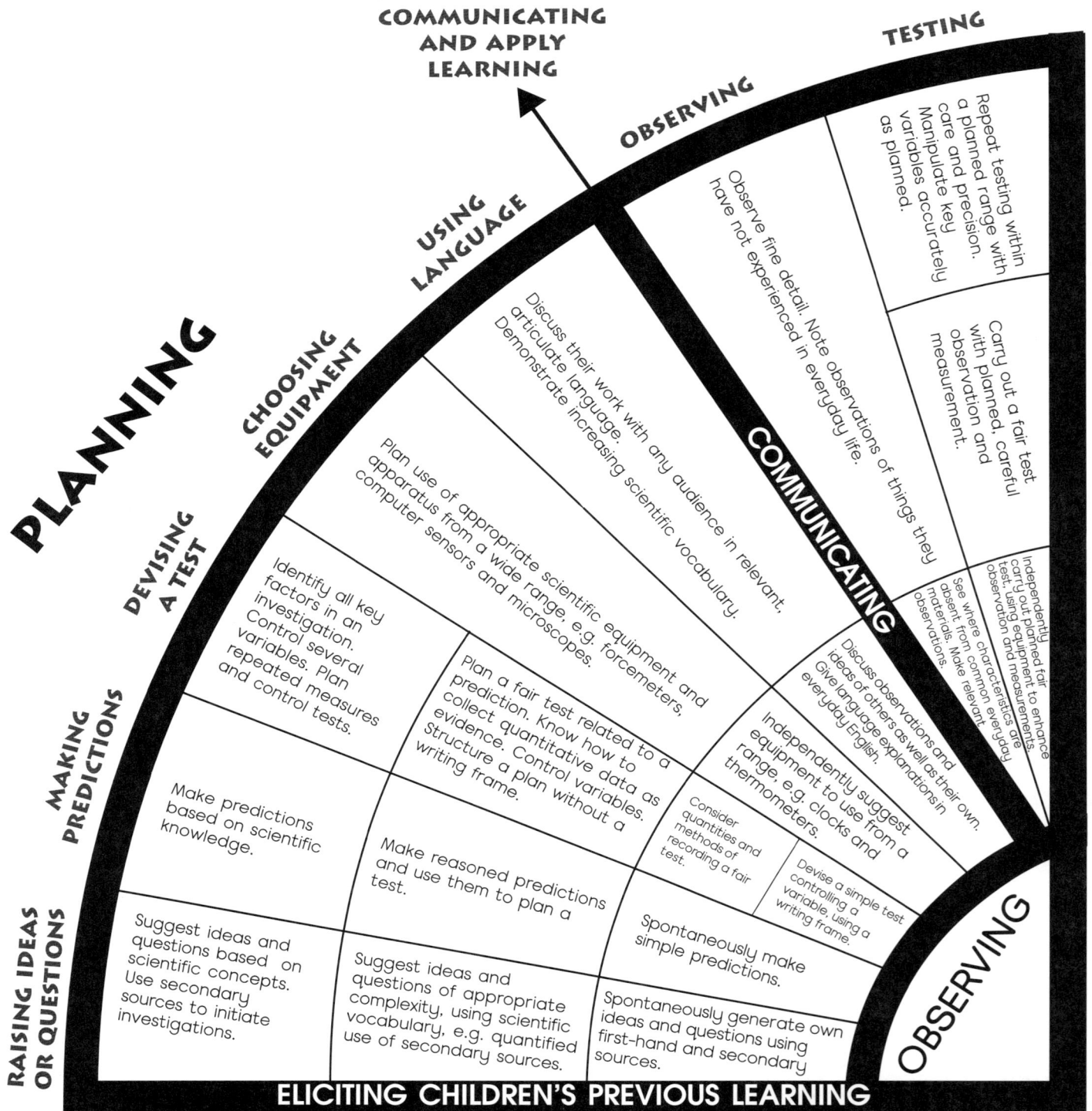

COMMUNICATING AND APPLY LEARNING

TESTING

OBSERVING

PLANNING

USING LANGUAGE

CHOOSING EQUIPMENT

DEVISING A TEST

MAKING PREDICTIONS

RAISING IDEAS OR QUESTIONS

COMMUNICATING

OBSERVING

Repeat testing within a planned range with care and precision. Manipulate key variables accurately as planned.

Carry out a fair test with planned, careful observation and measurement.

Independently plan a fair test. Using equipment and measurements to enhance carry out planned observation and measurements.

Observe fine detail. Note observations of things they have not experienced in everyday life.

See where characteristics are absent from common everyday materials. Make relevant observations.

Discuss their work with any audience in relevant, articulate language. Demonstrate increasing scientific vocabulary.

Discuss observations and ideas of others as well as their own. Give language explanations in everyday English.

Plan use of appropriate scientific equipment and apparatus from a wide range, e.g. forcemeters, computer sensors and microscopes.

Independently suggest equipment to use from a range, e.g. clocks and thermometers.

Identify all key factors in an investigation. Control several variables. Plan repeated measures and control tests.

Plan a fair test related to a prediction. Know how to collect quantitative data as evidence. Control variables. Structure a plan without a writing frame.

Consider quantities and methods of recording a fair test.

Devise a simple test controlling a variable, using a writing frame.

Make predictions based on scientific knowledge.

Make reasoned predictions and use them to plan a test.

Spontaneously make simple predictions.

Suggest ideas and questions based on scientific concepts. Use secondary sources to initiate investigations.

Suggest ideas and questions of appropriate complexity, using scientific vocabulary, e.g. quantified use of secondary sources.

Spontaneously generate own ideas and questions using first-hand and secondary sources.

ELICITING CHILDREN'S PREVIOUS LEARNING

5
Without support children:

4
With very little support children:

3
With limited support children:

EXPLORING

ACTIVE STARTING POINT THROUGH

PRESENTING EVIDENCE

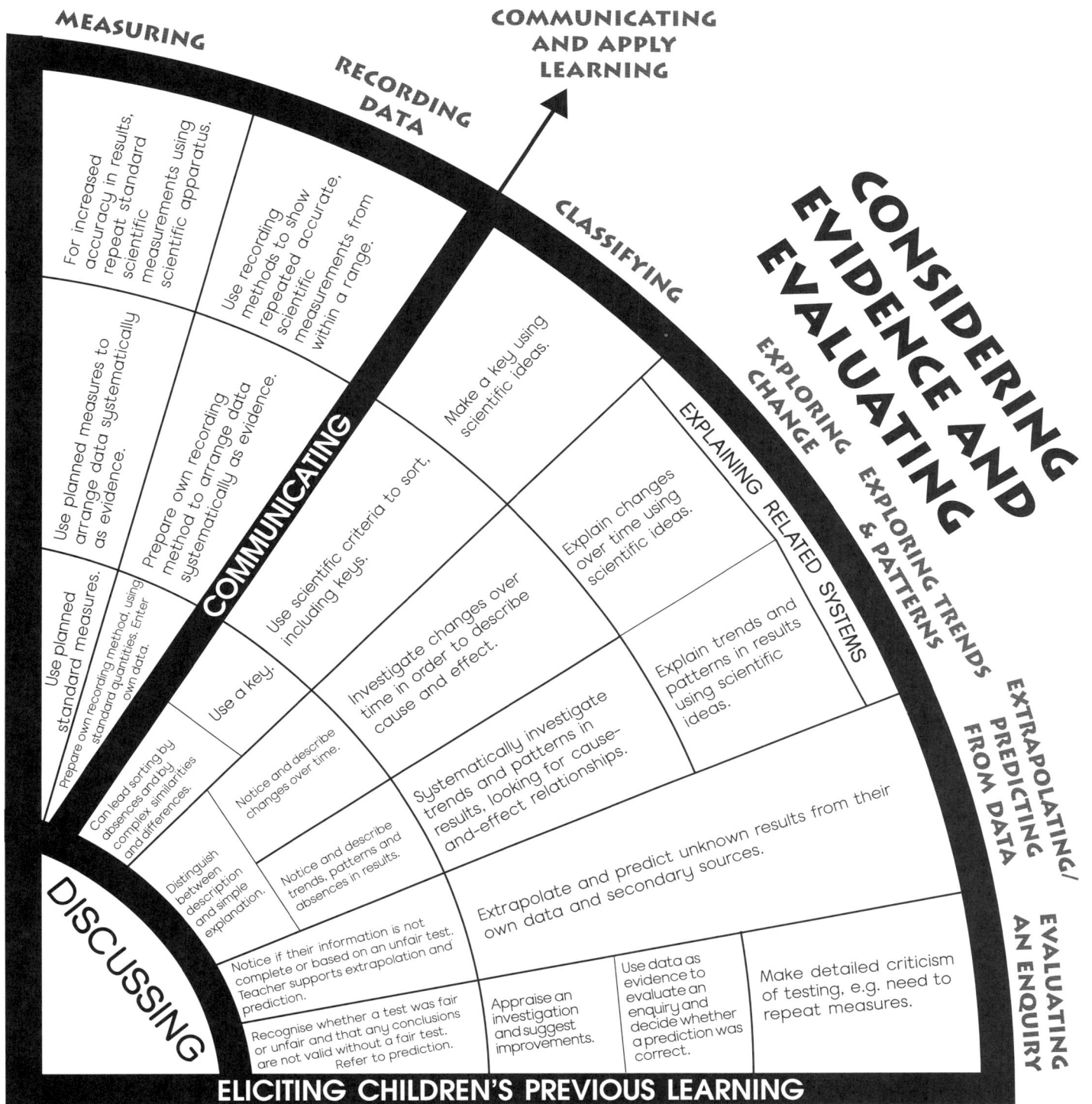

MEASURING

COMMUNICATING AND APPLY LEARNING

RECORDING DATA

CLASSIFYING

CONSIDERING EVIDENCE AND EVALUATING

EXPLORING CHANGE

EXPLORING TRENDS & PATTERNS

EXPLAINING RELATED SYSTEMS

EXTRAPOLATING/ PREDICTING FROM DATA

EVALUATING AN ENQUIRY

COMMUNICATING

For increased accuracy in results, repeat standard scientific measurements using scientific apparatus.

Use recording methods to show repeated accurate, scientific measurements from within a range.

Use planned measures to arrange data systematically as evidence.

Prepare own recording method to arrange data systematically as evidence.

Make a key using scientific ideas.

Use planned standard measures.

Prepare own recording method, using standard quantities. Enter own data.

Use scientific criteria to sort, including keys.

Explain changes over time using scientific ideas.

Can lead sorting by absences and by complex similarities and differences.

Use a key.

Investigate changes over time in order to describe cause and effect.

Explain trends and patterns in results using scientific ideas.

Distinguish between description and simple explanation.

Notice and describe changes over time.

Systematically investigate trends and patterns in results, looking for cause-and-effect relationships.

Notice and describe trends, patterns and absences in results.

Extrapolate and predict unknown results from their own data and secondary sources.

Notice if their information is not complete or based on an unfair test. Teacher supports extrapolation and prediction.

Recognise whether a test was fair or unfair and that any conclusions are not valid without a fair test. Refer to prediction.

Appraise an investigation and suggest improvements.

Use data as evidence to evaluate an enquiry and decide whether a prediction was correct.

Make detailed criticism of testing, e.g. need to repeat measures.

DISCUSSING

ELICITING CHILDREN'S PREVIOUS LEARNING

3
With limited support children:

4
With very little support children:

5
Without support children:

REFLECTING

FIRST-HAND OR SECONDARY SOURCES

7

PROGRESSION GRIDS

The grids on these pages summarise the range of levels you are likely to find in Year 6. The grid on these two pages describes the characteristics of a child working at Level 3 and the teaching strategies that will help them to move on to working at Level 4.

Progression through the skills of scientific enquiry will involve children in increasing:
- quantification
- fairness
- rigour
- independence
- focus
- awareness of the processes they are undertaking.

There is a general progression towards children's autonomy in the use of enquiry skills. Initially, the teacher leads the children. Then, the teacher will model the process, for example by using the correct language to describe what they are doing. With further development, the children begin to apply the skills in familiar contexts with limited support. Ultimately, they will take the lead and become independent. At this stage the use of pupil sheets to structure planning and testing should not be necessary and could limit further development.

Grid A

Features of child at Level 3

Planning
Children respond to suggestions and put forward their own ideas as to how to find out the answer to a question and how to carry out an enquiry. They raise their own questions with teacher support. They recognise why it is important to test ideas. When asked, they offer sensible predictions for a test not yet attempted. They use suitable texts and ICT to find information related to their enquiry. Standard measures are planned with teacher support.

Obtaining and presenting evidence
Children make relevant observations, including where features are absent in common everyday contexts. They measure quantities, such as mass and length, and safely use a range of simple equipment, such as clocks, simply calibrated scales and thermometers. Familiar equipment is selected by the children. Standard measures are used independently.

With some help, the children make a fair comparison, recognising and explaining why it is fair. They independently record their observations in a variety of ways, including in tables, block graphs and pictograms. Teacher support is needed for axes and scales. They communicate, with the use of appropriate scientific vocabulary, what they have found from their work. They follow complex instructions independently and use ICT where appropriate.

Considering evidence and evaluating
Children provide explanations for observations and, where they occur, for simple patterns in recorded measurements. They communicate, with the use of appropriate scientific vocabulary, what they have found out from their work, and suggest how tests could be improved. They indicate whether evidence supports any prediction made.

Lead explanations of what is happening in terms of scientific language and understanding. Use ICT where appropriate.

Teaching strategies to move child on to Level 4	Features of child at Level 4
Use a wider variety of active starting points to encourage children's questions. These could include interacting with texts (including newspaper articles, fiction and poetry), diary keeping (e.g. plotting plant growth), card sorts (e.g. 'Are these solids, liquids or gases?'), making their own concept maps, looking at classification keys, watching videos, using CD-ROMs, educational visits, spreadsheets (e.g. data, collected by another class, on the number of dandelions in different habitats), posters and photographs. Include information in graphic, tabular and diagrammatic forms. Start to move children on to planning for themselves, including result presentation. Use questions such as, 'Can you make a plan to...?' and 'How can you make your test fair?' Teach the principle of factors by identifying them in a test. Lead the children in manipulating the factors. Ask children to describe a fair test accurately, and take what they say literally (e.g. take the temperature immediately if they have not specified an amount of time to wait). Take one variable at a time and manipulate it in ways the children suggest. Then let them plan their own test independently in a simple context.	**Planning** Children recognise when a fair test is an appropriate enquiry and describe, or show in the way in which they perform their task, how to vary one factor while keeping all others the same. They raise their own questions. Where appropriate, they make independent predictions. They select sources of information suitable for their purpose, independently plan the accurate use of standard measures and use ICT where appropriate.
Encourage the children to use their skills in standard measurement to plan with increasing accuracy. Insist they incorporate sensible predictions in their plan, and do not make them as they carry out the test. The contexts for their work should become increasingly scientific and their plans should be developed from previous knowledge and experience. (e.g. 'I know what circuits are and that batteries can be used together. Will adding more batteries to a circuit make a bulb brighter?') Children should select their equipment from an increasing range. They need free access to rulers, scales, timers and thermometers with a range of calibration. Introduce them to new forms of measurement using microscopes, forcemeters, and computer sensors of light, heat and sound. Encourage repeated and accurate measurement as good practice. Initially, children will need your support to arrange their data systematically, but they will improve with practice. They should use a range of appropriate methods to present their evidence clearly.	**Obtaining and presenting evidence** Children recognise and assess possible hazards and risks to themselves and to others when working with living things and materials. They select suitable equipment to use safely, make a series of observations and use standard measurements that are adequate for the task. They can observe fine detail, even in non-familiar contexts. They use complex equipment, such as forcemeters and microscopes. They record their observations and measurements independently and present them clearly as evidence, using drawings, diagrams, tables and bar charts. With teacher support, they begin to plot points of a simple graph. They use ICT where appropriate.
After a test, ask questions such as: 'Was it a fair test?' 'How did you make it a fair test?' 'How can you change it to make it fairer?' Once the testing process has been reviewed, the children should be encouraged to analyse the data to find patterns independently. They should be taught how to look for trends. Encourage them to relate ideas to previous work, and to their developing scientific ideas and language. They should state whether evidence collected supported any prediction made in their plan. If the evidence differs from the prediction, how does it do so? Help children reject an idea in the light of evidence.	**Considering evidence and evaluating** Children use their graphs and tables to point out and interpret patterns in their data, using ICT where appropriate. They begin to relate their conclusions to these patterns and to scientific knowledge and understanding, and communicate them using appropriate scientific language. They indicate whether the evidence collected supports any prediction made. They suggest ways in which their work could be improved.

PROGRESSION GRIDS

The grid on these two pages describes the characteristics of a child working at Level 4 and the teaching strategies that will help them to move on to working at Level 5.

Progression through the skills of scientific enquiry will involve children in increasing:

◆ quantification
◆ fairness
◆ rigour
◆ independence
◆ focus
◆ awareness of the processes they are undertaking.

There is a general progression towards children's autonomy in the use of enquiry skills. Initially, the teacher leads the children. Then, the teacher will model the process, for example by using the correct language to describe what they are doing. With further development, the children begin to apply the skills in familiar contexts with limited support. Ultimately, they will take the lead and become independent. At this stage the use of pupil sheets to structure planning and testing should not be necessary and could limit further development.

Grid B

Features of child at Level 4

Planning
Children recognise when a fair test is an appropriate enquiry and describe, or show in the way in which they perform their task, how to vary one factor while keeping all others the same. They raise their own questions. Where appropriate, they make independent predictions. They select sources of information suitable for their purpose, independently plan the accurate use of standard measures and use ICT where appropriate.

Obtaining and presenting evidence
Children recognise and assess possible hazards and risks to themselves and to others when working with living things and materials. They select suitable equipment to use safely, make a series of observations and use standard measurements that are adequate for the task. They can observe fine detail, even in non-familiar contexts. They use complex equipment, such as forcemeters and microscopes. They record their observations and measurements independently and present them clearly as evidence, using drawings, diagrams, tables and bar charts. With teacher support, they begin to plot points of a simple graph. They use ICT where appropriate.

Considering evidence and evaluating
Children use their graphs and tables to point out and interpret patterns in their data, using ICT where appropriate. They begin to relate their conclusions to these patterns and to scientific knowledge and understanding, and communicate them using appropriate scientific language. They indicate whether the evidence collected supports any prediction made. They suggest ways in which their work could be improved.

Teaching strategies to move child on to Level 5	Features of child at Level 5
Help children to divide questions into those that require the use of a secondary source, those that are testable through investigation, and others. Then discuss how to select a style of enquiry. Model the use of appropriate secondary sources as research tools and use skills, such as those outlined in the Literacy Framework, to make appropriate selections. Where questions are open to investigation, require children to plan their single factors rigorously. Then work alongside them to list and prioritise a limited number of key factors based on their scientific knowledge and understanding. Discuss how to control these key factors, with a view to the children eventually controlling them independently in their testing. Accurate and repeated measurements should be expected. Support this skill by modelling the use of measurements.	**Planning** Children identify what kind of enquiry is appropriate in order to try to answer a question. They select from a range of sources of information. In contexts that involve only a few factors, they consider key factors in planning a fair test. Where appropriate, they make predictions based on their scientific knowledge and understanding. They select apparatus for a range of tasks and plan to use it safely. Repeated accurate measurements are planned within a range. They use ICT where appropriate.
Teacher-produced pro-formas should not be used by these children as they are required to see planning as an integral part of their investigation. The contexts can be complex and you may introduce more abstract ideas such as thermal conduction. Predictions made by this group sound more like hypotheses and so the children can be introduced to the hypothesis as a concept. They select their own apparatus and can be introduced to apparatus that measures an abstract idea, such as an ammeter measuring current. They use a sophisticated range of recording methods to present their quantitative data systematically and appropriately as evidence. They need to be taught how to produce a scatter graph and a line graph with the y axes dependent on changes in the x axis. Graphic, tabular, diagrammatic and written records can be produced using word-processing software, spreadsheets and databases. Encourage the children to check for anomalies, and stress that accurate repeated measurements will help them avoid mistakes.	**Obtaining and presenting evidence** Children make a series of observations, comparisons or standard measurements with precision appropriate to the task. They begin to repeat observations and measurements, and to offer simple explanations for any differences they encounter. New scientific apparatus is introduced. They record observations and measurements systematically and present data as a line graph or, with given axes and scales, as a scatter graph, where appropriate. Repeated measurements are made within a planned range. They use a range of units, appropriate scientific language and conventions to communicate quantitative and qualitative data. They use ICT where appropriate.
Provide evidence from another group and ask children to look for patterns and trends. Children should write questions to support other children who are checking their own results. For example, 'At what time was our unusual temperature reading taken?' Introduce the idea of inferential questions, for example 'Which factors do you think were crucial in influencing the number of tall plants found in different habitats?' Later, children ask each other inferential questions to validate their results. Encourage children to form a conclusion either orally or in writing to evaluate working methods, and ask what children now think in the light of evidence.	**Considering evidence and evaluating** Children draw conclusions that are consistent with the evidence and begin to relate these to scientific knowledge and understanding. They independently look for trends and patterns in data. They indicate whether the evidence collected supports any prediction made. They evaluate their working methods and use ICT where appropriate.

LESSON PLANS

The lesson plans give specific examples of how work in scientific enquiry can be focused to develop children's skills at the different levels. They are laid out in the following way.

Skills to be developed.

The lesson context identifies the aspects of the QCA Scheme of Work that are the focus of the investigation.

Learning objectives for the lesson derived from the QCA Scheme of Work.

A summary of how work can be differentiated for different ability groups.

Resources needed, and information about the timing of the lesson and the suggested groupings. It may be necessary to spread extended investigations over more than one session. The time allocated is to be divided at the discretion of the teacher.

The variation in timing between the lesson plans is deliberate and reflects the differing demands of the activities.

The introductory phase of the lesson. Italic text indicates possible teacher questions and instructions during the lesson.

The main activity. Information is provided on how the work may be differentiated, depending on whether children are moving from Level 3 to Level 4, or from Level 4 to Level 5.

FORCES IN ACTION

Measuring
Recording data (tables and line graphs)
Exploring trends and patterns from data

Extrapolating and predicting from data
Evaluating an enquiry
Risk analysis and control

Lesson context The children should be taught that the amount a rubber band stretches depends on the force acting on it.

Learning objectives *The children should learn how to:*
- make careful measurements of length
- represent data in a line graph and use this to identify patterns in data
- repeat measures and check them
- evaluate repeated measures.

Differentiation By outcome.

Requirements **Resources** Range of rubber bands of different thickness and length, masses with way of attaching to rubber bands, some attached, tape measures, graph paper, OHTs to contrast graphs, Pupil Sheet 7.

Timing 10-minute starting point.
60-minute activity.
10-minute discussion.

Suggested grouping Whole class for starting point then interest groups for activity. Whole class for discussion.

Starting point – *How many ways can you sort these rubber bands?*
Allow 1 minute, then get responses.

Remind the children that weight is a force and that it is measured in newtons.
Look at these rubber bands with weight on them.
– *How could we make a fair test of how much they stretch with a weight?*
– *What would we have to change and what should we keep the same?*
– *How could we record our answers to help show any patterns in the data?*
– *How can we keep the test safe?*

Children may suggest:
– will all long rubber bands stretch by the same amount?
– will all thick rubber bands stretch by the same amount?
– can all rubber bands stretch the same distance before they break?
– what is the maximum weight an rubber band can support?

Tell the children that they will need to use a forcemeter to find the weight of the different masses they will be adding to the end of their rubber bands.

Activity *The focus of this work is on your measurement so that you can analyse it for any patterns you can find. Consider what you will change and what you will keep the same and how you will record your measurements.*

Pupils plan and carry out their test.
As they are planning and testing, discuss with them the importance of repeating measurements to improve reliability.

– *Sometimes we can get different readings from each other. How can we improve our measuring?*
  (By repeating measurements.)
– *How can we use that idea in this test?*
– *Why is it important to repeat measurements?*

24

12

❷ – Children working at Level 3.
❸ – Children working at Level 4.
❹ – Children working at Level 5.

A plenary session in which discussion of findings, or evaluation of progress, may take place.

Different investigations will require different types of graph. Children who are comparing the extension of different rubber bands with the same weight will need to use bar charts. Children who are measuring the extension of one rubber band with several weights will need line graphs. Several bands could be plotted using line graphs on the same set of axes.

I'll remind you about line graphs. The variable on the X-axis is the one you are changing. This must be shown as numbers, for example … .
Force on the X-axis and length on the Y-axis is the correct way around if the graph is to show whether the greater the force the longer the band.
Draw your graph. Deliberately miss out one answer to try out on another group.

All groups put line graphs onto OHTs. Children who finish quickly should work on Pupil Sheet 7.

Review OHTs:
– *Did any result surprise you?*
– *Did the graph help you to spot a trend? What was the trend, summarised in a sentence?*
– *Which type of rubber band is the best?*

Discussion

What to look for

How evidence of children's attainment at the end of the work links to National Curriculum levels.

Children	typically
❸ working at **Level 3**	select an appropriate number of rubber bands for their test measure forces with a forcemeter and present measurements in tables produce a block graph of changes in length for different bands or, with help, produce a line graph of the changes on one band propose a relationship, such as a thin rubber band will stretch further say how their test was fair
❹ working at **Level 4**	plan to collect evidence as data for one variable in regular steps (for example 1N, 2N, 3N, 4N) record stretch in millimetres plan and carry out repeated measurements of one band present measurements in simple line graphs or bar charts if more appropriate and identify patterns in these evaluate explanations
❺ working at **Level 5**	use mean/median results of repeated measurements check that the band returns to its original length

Extending the approach

The lesson plan could be adapted to the following scientific contexts.

– When an object is submerged in water, the water provides an upward force (upthrust) on it.
– Use tables to present results, identifying patterns and drawing conclusions.
– Air resistance slows moving objects.
– When an object falls, air resistance acts in the opposite direction to the weight.
– Interpret a line graph and use it to describe the motion of spinners falling

Opportunities for extending the approach used in the lesson to further scientific knowledge, understanding and skill.

Cross-curricular links

Numeracy
Recording measurements accurately in newtons.
Recording data of rubber band stretch with different weights and times taken for differently weighted spinners to fall. Finding the mode and range in the data.
Drawing a line graph to represent a series of measurements of the lengths of the rubber band (Y-axis) with different weights attached (X-axis) or the weight of paper clips (X-axis) on time taken for a spinner to drop (Y-axis) and exploring trends.
Making predictions from the data and extrapolating patterns.

25

Links to other curriculum areas that are possible with this unit.

INTERDEPENDENCE AND ADAPTATION

Classifying

Lesson context

The children should be taught to use keys to identify animals and plants in a local habitat.

Learning objectives

The children should learn how to:
● make comparisons and identify simple patterns or associations in their own observations.

Differentiation

By outcome in skills development.

Requirements

Resources ICT sorting package, range of commercially produced keys set out as lists and branches, six contrasting plants labelled with names sufficient for each group, enlarged version of Pupil Sheet 1.

Timing 30-minute starting point.
20-minute activity.
15-minute discussion.

Suggested grouping Whole class for starting point, then mixed–ability groups of four for activity. Whole class for discussion.

Starting point

You have all visited different habitats.
– *What does 'habitat' mean?*
– *In what ways do habitats differ from one another?*
– *You went looking for living things – what living things did you find there?*
Check that they have remembered that plants are living things.

– *What do living things need?*
– *Plants need … .*
– *Animals need … .*
Collect ideas.

*Plants and animals are suited to their habitat and are different from the plants and animals found in another habitat. Scientists have to know what plant or animal they are looking at. They have developed a way of recording what they see. It is called a key. It is **not** like a door key or even a key that you put on a map or graph. It is a way of asking questions to which you can only answer yes or no, or sometimes questions that will split one group into several other groups.*

Look at these two plants. Can anyone think of a question, the answer to which would be yes for one plant and no for the other?
Collect suggestions.

Challenge answers that are ambiguous or unclear, for example 'Is it tall?' Challenge the children to explain how the question could be tightened to include a quantity 'Is it taller than 15cm?' *Scientists try to think of questions that won't change so maybe height isn't a good one as plants grow. Look for differences in the plants, use the lenses.*

Children may suggest:
– leaf size, arrangement, position, number, shape
– stem rigidity, pattern, cross section, sappiness
– flower size, arrangement, position, number, shape
– root length
– hairiness.

Collect ideas and write them down under headings of leaf, stem, flower, roots.

Pupil Sheet 1 shows you a way of recording your key.
Use enlarged version of Pupil Sheet 1 or (better) the circles chalked on the playground.

Look at these six children. Think of a question that will separate them that will always be true.
We are looking for positive, measureable aspects.
Collect ideas, for example, *Does the child have fair hair?*

Choose one and write it in the centre of the circle. Pupils move outwards one pace, either to the left if they answer yes or to the right if they answer no. Choose one subset of the children and ask a question about them to subdivide them. Track them to the next layer out in the concentric circles. Write the questions in the relevant sector as you go. When you are down to one child write their name in their exclusive sector. Keep asking questions, writing them down and moving the children until they are all in their own exclusive sector.

I am thinking of a child in this group. You have to ask me questions to identify them.
– *What was our first question?* (Read from centre circle.)
This child answers no to that question.
Point to the sector they now have to look at and read its question. Answer the question yes or no and continue until the key reveals the child you were thinking of.

Activity

Put all of your plants in the centre circle.
Think of a question that will separate them.
Now carefully complete a key of your plants. Record all the different ways you had to sort them.

Discussion

Group A, choose one of your plants. Group B, ask questions using Group A's key to identify the plant they are thinking of.
Go around each group checking that their key works. Amend any mistakes.
Use this session to review the different types of key and to check that the children are able to use them.

What to look for

	Children	typically
❸	working at **Level 3**	group animals and plants by similarities and differences use questions in keys to help identify some plants and animals
❹ ❺	working at **Levels 4** and **5**	make and use scientific keys to identify plants and animals

— Cross-curricular links —

ICT
Writing flow charts of instructions.

Numeracy
Using the internet to search large databases and to interpret information.
Branching databases.

MICRO-ORGANISMS

Observing
Exploring trends and patterns
Risk analysis and control

Lesson context

The children should be taught that micro-organisms feed and grow.

Learning objectives

The children should learn how to:
- make suggestions about what yeast needs to grow
- make careful observations and compare them in order to draw conclusions about the effect of yeast on dough
- explain conclusions using scientific knowledge and understanding.

Differentiation

By outcome in skills development. ❸ supported by Pupil Sheet 2.

Requirements

Resources Live yeast, dough, method of heating water, apparatus for measuring capacity, small containers or film canisters and balloons or sealable plastic bags, thermometers, Pupil Sheet 2.

Timing 15-minute starting point.
20-minute planning activity plus activity carried out across a day of observations.
15-minute discussion.

Suggested grouping Whole class for starting point, then mixed-ability interest groups for activity (different groups involved in different parts of the bread-making process). Groups, then whole class for discussion.

Starting point

Use a bread-making activity as the basis for the following investigation. Ensure that the children are aware of the different ingredients, and in particular of the yeast and its food supply.

The yeast is a living thing. It is very small and is called a micro-organism. This means that, as with all living things, it grows and reproduces. As it grows it produces a gas which makes the dough rise.
- *What do you think it uses for food to grow?*
- *Why do you think the bread no longer rises when cooked?*
- *How would you know if it is producing gas?*

Children may suggest:
- its food comes from the other bread ingredients fat/water/sugar. We could isolate each one and see if it grows
- it no longer rises when the bread is cooked because the yeast is dead. Is it killed by heat?
- we could see if the gas will inflate something.

Note Using a balloon on the end of a test tube is one way this can be shown. Inflating a sealable plastic bag or using something like a film canister with a loosely fitting lid which will pop off are other possibilities.

- *What safety issues do we have to consider in this work?*

Put pupils in interest groups to test ideas fairly and safely, for example: with and without sugar/fat/water and in combination; measuring temperature of different places in bread; using water of different temperatures.

Plan your test, what you are going to observe and a table to record your results.
Pupils plan and carry out tests. ❸ children use Pupil Sheet 2 to support their planning.

Write five questions for another group to answer about your results. Summarise in a sentence what your results show.

Those who finish early can draw graphs, either bar charts for ❸ children or line graphs for ❹ and ❺ children. See page 21 for guidance on drawing a line graph.

Each group answers the other groups' questions. Share summary sentences as a whole class.

— *What can we say we have found out?*
Bread rises when it contains yeast but without yeast, dough does not rise. Yeast does not grow in cold or boiling water. It produces little gas without sugar. So the perfect conditions for growing yeast are sugary warm ones.

	Children	typically
❸	working at **Level 3**	suggest that sugar is food for yeast and plan a test to count bubbles of gas in testing, count the bubbles for an agreed time but add more sugar to same solution carry out this test fairly for one variable but do not control another (such as the temperature) generalise about what the evidence shows may have difficulty in interpreting another group's results
❹	working at **Level 4**	plan the test to control the variable (of, say, adding sugar) suggest a range of temperatures pertinent to the test use scientific knowledge of living things to predict they will grow when warm carry out the test fairly arrange data as evidence to check their initial prediction looks for trends and patterns in data in another group's work
❺	working at **Level 5**	change one variable in a systematic way, for example 20° differences in temperature or doubling sugar concentration in four tests may suggest the gas is carbon dioxide carry out regular sampling to provide evidence for a line graph interpret the line graph as evidence

Cross-curricular links

ICT
Graphing package, database.
Spreadsheet modelling.
Control and monitoring. What happens when ...?

Numeracy
Revisiting use of thermometer in setting up yeast growth experiments.
Using thermometers with increasing accuracy and complexity in scale reading.
Drawing time (Y-axis) versus area of gas production (X-axis) line graph.

MORE ABOUT DISSOLVING: 1

Eliciting children's previous learning
Making predictions
Risk analysis and control
Testing

Lesson context

The children should be taught:
- that solids which do not dissolve in water can be separated by filtering, which is similar to sieving
- that when solids dissolve a clear solution is formed (which may be coloured) and the solid cannot be separated by filtering
- that when the liquid evaporates from a solution the solid is left behind.

Learning objectives

The children should learn how to:
- describe a scientific process in a series of sequenced steps
- make predictions about which types of water contain dissolved materials and test these predictions
- make predictions about what happens when water from a solution evaporates and test these predictions.

Differentiation

By pupil sheet.

Requirements

Resources Safe heating source, pan, water, salt, blue ink, clean cold surface, Pupil Sheet 3, Pupil Sheet 4.

Timing **Session 1:** 30-minute starting point.
Session 2: 10-minute starting point. 15-minute activity. 15-minute discussion.

Suggested grouping **Session 1:** Whole class as individuals for starting point.
Session 2: Whole class for starting point. Mixed-ability pairs for activity. Whole class for discussion.

SESSION 1

Starting point

The cartoon in Pupil Sheet 3 can be used to elicit children's ideas about how to clean a dirty puddle **and** sea water, coloured ink, distilled water.

SESSION 2

Look at this water which I am adding salt to. I am going to boil it on the stove.
- *What issues of safety must you consider when heating?*
- *How will we know that the salt has dissolved?*
- *How long do you think it will take to boil? How will you know that it is boiling?*
- *When it boils how could we capture any water that is evaporating from the pan?*
Collect suggestions.

- *Why will it condense on a cold surface?*
- *Will the water that condenses be salty?*
- *Those who say yes, why do you think that? Those who say no, why do you think that?*
- *How will we know who is right?*
- *What safety issues do we have to consider?*
- *If we now try boiling blue ink do you think the condensed water we catch on the cold surface will be blue or not? Give a reason for your answer.*
- *Is it the same for dirty puddle water? How is that different from salty water and blue ink? Use scientific words to help you say it clearly.*

In supervised groups children carry out the test safely. (Others could be doing the suggested activities above.)

Write a sentence about predicting the type of water that will condense if a liquid is pure, has undissolved material in it, has dissolved material in it. Try to think of other examples you know, not the ones we tested. Use as much scientific vocabulary as you can.

❸ children should use Pupil Sheet 4. The others should design their own table.

Children	typically
❸ working at **Level 3**	predict that when an aqueous solution is heated, only water condenses and the dissolved solid remains in the container
❹ ❺ working at **Levels 4** and **5**	predict that when all the water has evaporated from an aqueous solution, the solid can be recovered from the container

Cross-curricular links

Literacy
Writing instructions.
Writing in sequence.

Numeracy
Suggesting suitable units and measuring equipment to estimate and measure capacity of liquid in condensing tests.
Recording estimates and readings to scales of 1ml(cm³) in 10ml(cm³) measuring cylinder.

ICT
Multimedia presentation.
Control and monitoring. What happens when ...?

MORE ABOUT DISSOLVING: 2

Raising ideas or questions
Devising a test
Choosing equipment
Observing and measuring

Recording data (line graph)
Exploring change
Exploring trends and patterns
Extrapolating and predicting from data

Lesson context

The children should be taught that some solids dissolve in water.

Learning objectives

The children should learn how to:

- turn ideas about helping solids dissolve more quickly into a form that can be investigated and decide how to carry out a fair test
- decide what apparatus to use and make careful observations and measurements
- make comparisons and draw conclusions
- use a line graph to present results
- know that several repeated measurements provide data that can be used with more confidence
- draw a line graph from results
- evaluate a graph in terms of how well it represents experimental data.

Differentiation

By outcome in skills development and Pupil Sheet 5 for ❸.

Note If this is the first time the children have focused on repeated measurements or line graphs they will need plenty of time to practise the relevant skills.

Requirements

Resources ICT graphing package, sugar (granulated, castor, muscavado, etc.), thermometer (non-mercury), apparatus for measuring volume, apparatus for taking mass of a solid, salt, timers, scoops for measuring amounts of solid, artificial sweetener, calculator, graph paper, OHTs and OHP, Pupil Sheet 5.

Timing **Session 1:** 20-minute starting point. 60-minute activity (plus 30-minute revision if necessary). 15-minute discussion.
Session 2: 15-minute starting point. 30-minute activity. 15-minute discussion.

Suggested grouping Whole class for starting points then mixed-ability interest groups for activities. Whole class for discussions.

SESSION 1

Starting point

We have looked a lot at dissolving. Your previous work gave some good examples.
Name children from previous discussion who thought of some different examples, otherwise suggest: sugar in a cup of tea.

There is a range of sugars. Does anyone know the names of any?
- *What ideas do you have about how to make materials dissolve as **quickly** as possible?*

Children may suggest:
- stirring
- the size of the particles of solid
- temperature of the water
- volume of water.
Write down ideas as they are suggested.

- *What tests can you think of to find out if stirring does make a difference to the speed the material dissolves? How can you make it fair?*

Children may suggest:
- try using the same amount of solids. *How could we measure the same amount of solid? Is there another way?* (Mass or volume)
- the same number of stirs
- the same volume of water
- varying the temperature of the water.

All of our ideas can be tested fairly. Decide which idea appeals to you.
Put pupils in interest groups to test out different ideas.

Activity

❸ children use Pupil Sheet 5 to plan the test. Carry out the test and present the results in a table.

Revise how to produce a line graph.
The scale on the X-axis is for the variable you are changing. This is the independent variable. It is shown as numbers.
Look at your table. What are you going to put on the X-axis?

This section of the graph is the Y-axis. The variable here is called the dependent variable. It changes as you alter the independent variable. You must be able to measure it.

Check that the children know how to plot points correctly.

Now draw your graph and be ready to give it to another group to analyse and present to the class.
Don't forget that the graph needs a title to tell other people what it is about.

Discussion

- *What was this group's question?*
- *How did they measure it?*
- *How do the X- and Y-axes relate to one another?*
- *What are the general trends and patterns?*
- *Do any results not fit the pattern? Why might they be different?*
To the group whose graph is being analysed: *Did you repeat your measures to check them? We will talk more about this in the next session.*

CONTINUED IN SESSION 2 (see page 22)

MORE ABOUT DISSOLVING: 2 – SESSION 2

CONTINUED FROM SESSION 1 (page 21)

CONTINUED FROM SESSION 1 (page 21)

We are going to find out how long sweeteners need to dissolve in water of different temperatures. I have got chilled water, water at room temperature, warm water and hot water. Each group is going to test how long it takes for the sweetener to dissolve at each temperature. Put the results in a table.

Starting point

Activity

Each group does the test and gets their results.
Look on the OHP.
- *What happened for each group with the chilled water?*
- *What happened with water at room temperature?*
- *What happened with warm water?*
- *What happened with hot water?*
Note results down on a table on an OHT.

Group A calculate the average time for the sweetener to dissolve and plot on a graph.
Group B plot all the individual times from each group at each temperature.
Children plot graphs and transfer these onto an OHT.

Discussion

- *What strikes you about these graphs?*
- *Are the results at one temperature spread out or close together?*
- *Which set of results would you trust most?*
It is interesting how different the results are when we have several measurements of the same thing. This is good practice in science.
- *Can you explain why?*
- *How does repeating measurements differ from fair testing?*

What to look for

	Children	typically
3	working at Level 3	investigate an aspect of dissolving using a fair test present results in a suitable table or graph
4	working at Level 4	present results obtained in a suitable graph, identify trends and explain what the results show
5	working at Level 5	present results in a line graph where appropriate explain that repeating measurements increases reliability identify and extrapolate trends

Cross-curricular links

ICT
Graphing package.

Numeracy
Suggesting suitable units and measuring equipment to estimate and measure capacity of liquid in evaporating, condensing, filtration and dissolving tests.
Recording estimates and readings to scales of 1ml (cm³) in 10ml (cm³) measuring cylinder.
Designing tabulation to show the mass of different solids dissolving in the same amount of water.
Producing line graph of tests to show salt (or another solid) dissolved faster when the water was hotter (Y-axis temperature and X-axis time). Line graph showing different sugars dissolving over time (Y-axis time and X-axis mass of solid).
Extrapolating a trend.
Reading off what might happen at intermediate values.
Extending curves of line graphs.

22

REVERSIBLE AND IRREVERSIBLE CHANGES

Classifying

The children should be taught about reversible changes.

Lesson context

The children should learn how to:
● classify changes as reversible and irreversible.

Learning objectives

By outcome of depth of links made.

Differentiation

Resources   Pupil Sheet 6.
Timing   30-minute activity.
                 30-minute discussion.

Requirements

Suggested grouping   Individuals for activity, then whole class for discussion.

When scientists are investigating, they must be clear about what they understand.
A concept map is a useful way of doing this. It can be used as a way of classifying things. You can use concept maps to help you sort out your ideas and think about investigations, or you can use them as a way of recording what you found out. It can be useful to do both, to see how your ideas have changed. A concept is an idea. A concept map links ideas together with arrows. We can write next to the arrows what the links are. We call the links 'facts'.

Starting point

Pupil Sheet 6 has a list of words you can use to construct a concept map about reversible and irreversible changes.
If you can think of real-life examples you can add or anything else to make it clearer please do so.
You have 30 minutes to do this because the thinking time is to allow you to plan how to arrange the words. There is no single correct concept map, it is to help you think about the issues.

Activity

Go through each word and collect a class example.
As we go through each word look at your concept map and add things to it.
– *Is it an irreversible change? How do you know?*
– *Is it a reversible change? How do you know?*
– *How would you reverse the change?*

Discussion

When all words have been discussed:
Check your concept maps for any mistakes. Cross them through. When you have finished, use your concept map as a revision card to remind you what we found out.

What to look for

	Children	typically
❸	working at **Level 3**	classify some simple changes, such as melting, as reversible and others, for example burning, as irreversible
❹	working at **Level 4**	classify some changes, such as dissolving, as reversible and state how to reverse the process classify other changes, for example burning, as irreversible think of plenty of real-life examples
❺	working at **Level 5**	explain that irreversible changes create new materials which can include gases and identify some evidence, for example vigorous bubbling, for the production of gas

FORCES IN ACTION

Measuring
Recording data (tables and line graphs)
Exploring trends and patterns from data

Extrapolating and predicting
  from data
Evaluating an enquiry
Risk analysis and control

Lesson context

The children should be taught that the amount a rubber band stretches depends on the force acting on it.

Learning objectives

The children should learn how to:
- make careful measurements of length
- represent data in a line graph and use this to identify patterns in data
- repeat measures and check them
- evaluate repeated measures.

Differentiation

By outcome.

Requirements

Resources Range of rubber bands of different thickness and length, masses with way of attaching to rubber bands, some attached, tape measures, graph paper, OHTs to contrast graphs, Pupil Sheet 7.

Timing 10-minute starting point.
60-minute activity.
10-minute discussion.

Suggested grouping Whole class for starting point then interest groups for activity. Whole class for discussion.

Starting point

– *How many ways can you sort these rubber bands?*
Allow 1 minute, then get responses.

Remind the children that weight is a force and that it is measured in newtons.
Look at these rubber bands with weight on them.
– *How could we make a fair test of how much they stretch with a weight?*
– *What would we have to change and what should we keep the same?*
– *How could we record our answers to help show any patterns in the data?*
– *How can we keep the test safe?*

Children may suggest:
– will all long rubber bands stretch by the same amount?
– will all thick rubber bands stretch by the same amount?
– can all rubber bands stretch the same distance before they break?
– what is the maximum weight an rubber band can support?

Tell the children that they will need to use a forcemeter to find the weight of the different masses they will be adding to the end of their rubber bands.

Activity

The focus of this work is on your measurement so that you can analyse it for any patterns you can find. Consider what you will change and what you will keep the same and how you will record your measurements.

Pupils plan and carry out their test.
As they are planning and testing, discuss with them the importance of repeating measurements to improve reliability.

– *Sometimes we can get different readings from each other. How can we improve our measuring?*
  (By repeating measurements.)
– *How can we use that idea in this test?*
– *Why is it important to repeat measurements?*

Different investigations will require different types of graph. Children who are comparing the extension of different rubber bands with the same weight will need to use bar charts. Children who are measuring the extension of one rubber band with several weights will need line graphs. Several bands could be plotted using line graphs on the same set of axes.

I'll remind you about line graphs. The variable on the X-axis is the one you are changing. This must be shown as numbers, for example … .
Force on the X-axis and length on the Y-axis is the correct way around if the graph is to show whether the greater the force the longer the band.
Draw your graph. Deliberately miss out one answer to try out on another group.

All groups put line graphs onto OHTs. Children who finish quickly should work on Pupil Sheet 7.

Review OHTs:
- *Did any result surprise you?*
- *Did the graph help you to spot a trend? What was the trend, summarised in a sentence?*
- *Which type of rubber band is the best?*

	Children	typically
❸	working at **Level 3**	select an appropriate number of rubber bands for their test measure forces with a forcemeter and present measurements in tables produce a block graph of changes in length for different bands or, with help, produce a line graph of the changes on one band propose a relationship, such as a thin rubber band will stretch further say how their test was fair
❹	working at **Level 4**	plan to collect evidence as data for one variable in regular steps (for example 1N, 2N, 3N, 4N) record stretch in millimetres plan and carry out repeated measurements of one band present measurements in simple line graphs or bar charts if more appropriate and identify patterns in these evaluate explanations
❺	working at **Level 5**	use mean/median results of repeated measurements check that the band returns to its original length

Extending the approach

The lesson plan could be adapted to the following scientific contexts.

- When an object is submerged in water, the water provides an upward force (upthrust) on it.
- Use tables to present results, identifying patterns and drawing conclusions.
- Air resistance slows moving objects.
- When an object falls, air resistance acts in the opposite direction to the weight.
- Interpret a line graph and use it to describe the motion of spinners falling

Cross-curricular links

Numeracy
Recording measurements accurately in newtons.
Recording data of rubber band stretch with different weights and times taken for differently weighted spinners to fall. Finding the mode and range in the data.
Drawing a line graph to represent a series of measurements of the lengths of the rubber band (Y-axis) with different weights attached (X-axis) or the weight of paper clips (X-axis) on time taken for a spinner to drop (Y-axis) and exploring trends.
Making predictions from the data and extrapolating patterns.

HOW WE SEE THINGS

Asking a question
Devising a test
Testing and measuring

Recording data (tables, line graphs)
Exploring change
Exploring trends and patterns

Lesson context

The children should be taught to identify factors which might affect the size and position of the shadow of an object.

Learning objectives

The children should learn how to:
● investigate how changing one factor causes a shadow to change
● consider trends in results and decide whether there are results which do not fit in the pattern
● check measurements by repeating them.

Differentiation

Support ❸ children to control a single variable.

Requirements

Resources Variety of torches, OHP, opaque, translucent and transparent objects (include objects like rulers and combs that give regularly spaced, measurable features), metre stick, tape measure, graph paper, protractor, Pupil Sheet 8.

Timing 10-minute starting point.
90-minute activity.
20-minute discussion.

Suggested grouping Mixed-ability groups for starting point and activity. Whole class for discussion.

Starting point

You have a variety of light sources and a range of objects with which to make shadows.
Spend 5 minutes exploring ways in which the shadow can be made to change.

Mixed-ability groups of four children use different light sources and different objects (see resources).

Activity

– *How did the shadows change?* (Discuss size, position, intensity.)
Look at your pupil sheet now and decide the variable you can change that will affect the shadow.
Pupils plan their own investigation using the first part of Pupil Sheet 8.

Children may suggest:
– how can a shadow be made to look smaller/bigger?
– does the size alter in a regular way if the distance from the screen is increased by 5cm jumps or is doubled?
– does the angle of the light source to the object affect the position of the shadow?
– which light source makes the most distinct shadow?
– how can a shadow be made darker?
– what happens when we make shadows with different materials?

– *How can you get a result that can be measured and recorded as a number?*
– *How could you show your results as relationships between measurements so that you can contrast what happens as you try a range of tests?*
– *Why is it important to repeat measurements?*

Pupils design their tables of results (see Pupil Sheet 8) and when ready carry out the test they have designed.
You may want to revise how to produce a line graph (see page 21).

- *What was this group's question?*
- *How did they measure it?*
- *How do the X- and Y-axes relate to one another?*
- *What are the general trends and patterns?*
- *Do any results not fit the pattern?*
- *Why might they be different?*

To the group whose graph is being analysed: *Did you repeat your measurements to check them?*

Discussion

What to look for

	Children	typically
❸	working at **Level 3**	suggest moving the position of the object/light source plan to measure distance from light to object in three positions select suitable equipment predict the effect of moving the light source nearer need support to produce a line graph carry out fair testing use the table to make a generalisation
❹	working at **Level 4**	identify a range of factors: distance from a light source to object, source of beam, angle of beam, material and shape of object, distance of object from screen control these factors investigate one factor fairly and organise the data as evidence select suitable objects with a measurable, regular shape to make repeated, accurate measurements independently produce a line graph with labelled axes predict intermediate values and identify results which do not fit the pattern explain results in terms of light travelling
❺	working at **Level 5**	investigate the numerical relationship between distance and shadow size measure systematically plot a line graph accurately repeat the whole experiment to check data use line graphs to illustrate the pattern between variables

Cross-curricular links

Numeracy
Working out relationship between size of shadow and distance from light source.
Filling in missing information in a graph to suggest possible size of a shadow made at an intermediate distance from the light source.

ICT
Spreadsheet modelling.

CHANGING CIRCUITS

Asking questions **Testing**
Making predictions **Observing**
Devising a test **Exploring change**
Choosing equipment

Lesson context

The children should be taught that the brightness of bulbs in a circuit can be changed by changing wires in a circuit.

Learning objectives

The children should learn how to:
- suggest a question to investigate, decide what to do and what equipment to use to test this
- make fair comparisons and draw conclusions.

Differentiation

By outcome in skills development.

Requirements

Resources Wires of different length, thickness, colour, material, core or flex (insulated or not/with or without crocodile clips), fuse wire, wire on reels with both ends accessible (this can produce a much longer run of wire than is otherwise practical), bulbs, bulb holders, crocodile clips, buzzers, batteries or power sources, tissue paper, light sensor, Pupil Sheet 9, Pupil Sheet 10.

Timing 25-minute starting point.
25-minute activity.
25-minute discussion.

Suggested grouping Whole class for starting point, then pairs with contrasting sets of wires (see resources) for activity and discussion.

Starting point

Look at these wires. On Pupil Sheet 9 list at least five differences.
Today we are going to investigate whether changing the wires in a circuit will change the brightness of the bulb.
- *Do you think any of these differences can affect how bright the bulb in the circuit will be?*

Children may suggest:
- do wires of different length affect the brightness?
- do wires of different thickness affect the brightness?
- does what the wire is made of make a difference?
- does having insulation around the wire make a difference?

Ask each group to identify one question that they will investigate, to predict the outcome and to record their prediction on Pupil Sheet 9.

- *How would we know if the bulb is brighter?*
Discuss ideas, for example how many layers of tissue paper the bulb can be seen through, use of a light sensor. Some children might suggest swapping the bulb for a buzzer or motor to make the effect easier to observe.

Devise a test of your prediction. List the equipment you will need to do the test.

Activity

Pupils carry out their own test.
Those who finish early can use alternative measures, for example the motor turning or buzzer sounding, and see if they get the same results.

28

– *What do you know now about how differences in wires affect bulb brightness that you didn't know before?*
– *Can anyone suggest why wire length and thickness affect bulb brightness?*
– *What generalisations can we make? The … er the wire the … er the bulb lights.*

Do the assessment exercise on Pupil Sheet 10.

	Children	typically
❸	working at **Level 3**	suggest a variable to test make a relevant prediction design and construct a circuit with contrasting wires to test fairly whether bulbs light more brightly or dimly compare the brightness of the bulb for the different wires and decide whether their prediction was correct
❹	working at **Level 4**	suggest effects of varying wires make measurements to compare brightness quantitatively, for example how many layers of paper the bulb can be seen through repeat activities to check measurements identify patterns in the data and explain the effects they observed
❺	working at **Level 5**	plan a quantitative basis for the circuit design, for example doubling wire length, or using one then two then three wires from a multi-flex cable, or using numerical light sensor data use trends and patterns in data to explain the changes in electrical flow in scientific terms describe differences between wires usually used for circuits and fuse wires, based on scientific understanding

Cross-curricular links

ICT
Using a light sensor.
Control and monitoring. What happens when ...?

Numeracy
Making a summary table of ways that components in a circuit change the brightness of bulbs.

ENQUIRY IN TECHNOLOGICAL AND ENVIRONMENTAL CONTEXTS: 1

Extrapolating and predicting from (an artefact)
Choosing equipment

Observing and testing
Exploring change
Evaluating an enquiry

Lesson context

The children should be taught to use scientific knowledge to identify significant features of an artefact to be designed.

Learning objectives

The children should learn how to:
- plan a suitable approach, for example creating a variety of designs and selecting the best fit for the design specification
- test out designs making a series of observations
- adjust designs in a systematic way in light of the evidence collected
- explain their designs using their scientific knowledge and understanding where possible
- evaluate the limitations of their own and others' designs.

Differentiation

By outcome in skills development and by Pupil Sheet 12 for ❸ children.

Requirements

Resources Range of one-way switches (toggle, bell press, morse code, slide, knife switch, tremble switch, tilt switch), wires, buzzers, lamps for circuit construction, aluminium foil, sponge, carpet or other soft insulating materials, Pupil Sheet 11, Pupil Sheet 12.
Note One-way switches only have one on and one off position. Commercially available switches often have a case that can be removed to see the mechanism.

Timing 15-minute starting point.
60-minute activity.
50-minute discussion (30-minute drawing, 15-minute presenting and 5-minute trying out best).

Suggested grouping Whole class then friendship groups of four with four contrasting switches for starting point. Friendship groups or individuals for activity. Same groups then whole class for discussion, in separate session if necessary.

Starting point

Show the children the switches.
Decide when they are in the on position.
- *What is happening in all of them to allow the electricity to flow?*
- *How could we use the aluminium foil to produce a similar effect?*
Your task is in groups to design and make a pressure pad burglar alarm.
Some children might achieve better results individually.

Burglar alarms are usually in the off position or they would be on all the time!
- *How could we use the coming together of a switch made from aluminium foil to be switched on only if a burglar is there?*
If no response: *It could be completed by being stepped on or sat on!*
In friendship groups design and build your burglar alarm.
Think about how to make sure the aluminium pieces touch and that they are normally kept apart.
I have provided you with a range of equipment. If something you need is not available please ask.

Beware, buzzers are tricky. They work only if they are in the circuit the right way round.
Demonstrate a circuit with a buzzer wired in the wrong way around.
- *Is this a viable circuit, has it everything it needs? Does it work?*
Watch what happens when I put the buzzer in the other way around.
Change direction of flow through the buzzer by disconnecting it and reconnecting it in the same position but with the wires in opposite places.

Use Pupil Sheet 11 to help you to design and test your burglar alarm.
Pupils design their burglar alarms.

You were asked to think about how to make sure the aluminium pieces touch and that they are normally kept apart. How does your design do that?
If necessary: *Use the sponge like the filling in a sandwich; make your sponge like a mint with a hole in the middle; use the foil like bread on either side of the sponge sandwich.*

As they test their ideas: How was the sponge of different depths?
– How did you make it strong so that it would hold together?

When you are pleased with your design draw a diagram or cartoon sequence, to show how it developed.
Pupil Sheet 12 will help to sequence ideas for ❸ children. Others should present their annotated diagram on a large sheet.

In your groups make your own pupil sheet tell the story of how your burglar alarm developed from your original design to how it looks now.
Use the boxes to draw a picture and the space to write a sentence.
Try to explain clearly what the thinking was behind making the change and whether or not it worked.
Pupils draw a cartoon or annotated diagram.

In pairs of groups, the children present their work to one another. Each should declare a winner from the pair. Then compare that with another pair. Get two winning alarms and use them to catch out an unsuspecting 'burglar', for example the class teacher from next door.

	Children	typically
❸	working at **Level 3**	put forward ideas of what needs to be done to answer a question and, with help, plan what to do make relevant observations and record these appropriately suggest explanations for their observations and communicate these using scientific language
❹	working at **Level 4**	suggest how to investigate a question and plan what to do make a series of observations relevant to the task and record these appropriately interpret their data and relate this to scientific knowledge and understanding suggest how what they did could have been improved
❺	working at **Level 5**	plan what to do and how to use available resources effectively suggest limitations of the product made and how these could be reduced

Cross-curricular links

Numeracy
Tabulating pressure pad observations.
Diagram of burglar alarm.
Evaluating enquiries into burglar alarm design.

Design Technology
Evaluating design.

ICT
Controlling devices.

ENQUIRY IN TECHNOLOGICAL AND ENVIRONMENTAL CONTEXTS: 2

Raising ideas or questions
Devising a test and observing
Testing and measuring
Recording data (tables)

Exploring change
Exploring trends and patterns
Language
Evaluating an enquiry

Lesson context

This unit is intended to be investigative. It offers the opportunity for children to perform complete investigations.

Learning objectives

The children should learn how to:
- ask scientific questions
- plan how to answer questions
- decide what kind of evidence to collect
- collect and record data appropriately
- look critically at data collected and identify and describe patterns
- try to explain their results using their scientific knowledge and understanding
- describe the limitations of their own and others' evidence.

Differentiation

By outcome in skills development.

Requirements

Resources Dandelion plants from two locations, one with long and one with short grass, tape measures, area with long and short grass safe for pupils to visit, Pupil Sheet 13.

Timing 45-minute starting point.
30-minute activity.
30-minute poster design.
20-minute discussion.
Additional time is needed to design an ICT database, input data and interrogate the data.

Suggested grouping Whole class for starting point, then interest groups for activity and poster design. Whole class for discussion.

Starting point

Look at the dandelions. Sort them in as many ways as you can.
– What differences did you find?

Children may suggest:
- they are longer/shorter
- they have greener/more yellow stems
- they have larger/smaller flowers
- they have leaves of different size and shape.

Some of these were found in long grass and some in short grass.
– What predictions would you have made using your knowledge of what plants need to grow as to where the different plants were picked from?

Children may suggest:
- the longer ones/yellow stems/bigger leaves needed to grow higher to get more light in long grass
- the larger flowers are produced by short healthy plants in short grass.

Record the ideas as they are suggested.

Before you go into groups to plan your test I want us to consider what makes a fair test sample.
– Would one dandelion in each area give us good evidence? Why not?
– How many will be enough?
– Will just testing one area of long grass and one area of short grass give strong enough information?
You will be given credit for making your test as rigorous as possible; this will include other detailed observations of your plants, not just the one that you are addressing in your question.
Choose the question you are most interested in.
– Who wants to do question A/B/C, etc.?
Now get into the groups answering your question.
All members of the group need to fill in their own pupil sheet or computer database.

If more than four pupils want to answer a question, subdivide the group.
Pupils complete Pupil Sheet 13, with or without using a computer database.

Pupils go outside and collect their data, and record it in their groups.

Activity

If possible, interrogate the database for details of trends and patterns in data.

Discussion

Draw a poster to show your question, plans and results and write in large print a sentence to sum up your findings.
– What is your evidence showing?
– How do you know?
– How could it be shown clearly to another group?
– Have you got enough evidence for your conclusion to be reliable?

Pupils design posters.
– Look at this sentence. Can anyone suggest what is good about the way it sums up the evidence?
– Is it using good evidence with detailed observations and measurements?
– Do you agree with their scientific idea about why the evidence shows this?
– Is there a way their sentence can be improved to say more precisely what the test shows?
– How could the test be further developed to provide a better sample size?
If necessary: You only looked at ten leaves in each place so can you say leaves are longer in long grass than in short grass?
– How do you know it wasn't because one place was more in the shade?

Take all groups in turn. Provide less support in the analysis as you go to encourage pupil independence in describing the limitations of evidence.

Children	typically
❸ working at **Level 3**	put forward ideas of what needs to be done to answer a question and, with help, plan what to do
	make relevant observations and measurements and record these appropriately
	suggest explanations for their observations and communicate these using scientific language
❹ working at **Level 4**	make a suggestion of how to investigate a question and plan what to do
	make a series of observations or measurements relevant to the task and record these appropriately
	interpret their data and relate this to scientific knowledge and understanding
	suggest how what they did could have been improved
❺ working at **Level 5**	plan what to do and how to use available resources effectively
	suggest limitations of the data collected and how these could be reduced

Extending the approach

There are many other environmental investigations that can use this basic format of sessions and address similar learning objectives, such as the following.

Do you find more small insects on the top or the underside of leaves?
Is there any difference in the length and width of leaves on the top, middle or bottom of a shrub?
Will we find different kinds of animals if we take a sample of water from the top, middle and bottom of our school pond?

Cross-curricular links

Numeracy
Measuring the length of leaves (in mm).
Tabulating dandelion data.
Identifying trends and patterns in data of dandelions growing in two different locations. Looking critically at the results to decide how strongly they show a trend, particularly in relation to sample size.
Describing limitations of their dandelion investigation.
Evaluating enquiries into dandelion distribution.

ICT
Data handling package.
Analysing data and asking questions using complex sentences.
Evaluating information, checking accuracy and questioning plausibility.
Introduction to spreadsheet.
Monitoring environmental conditions and changes.

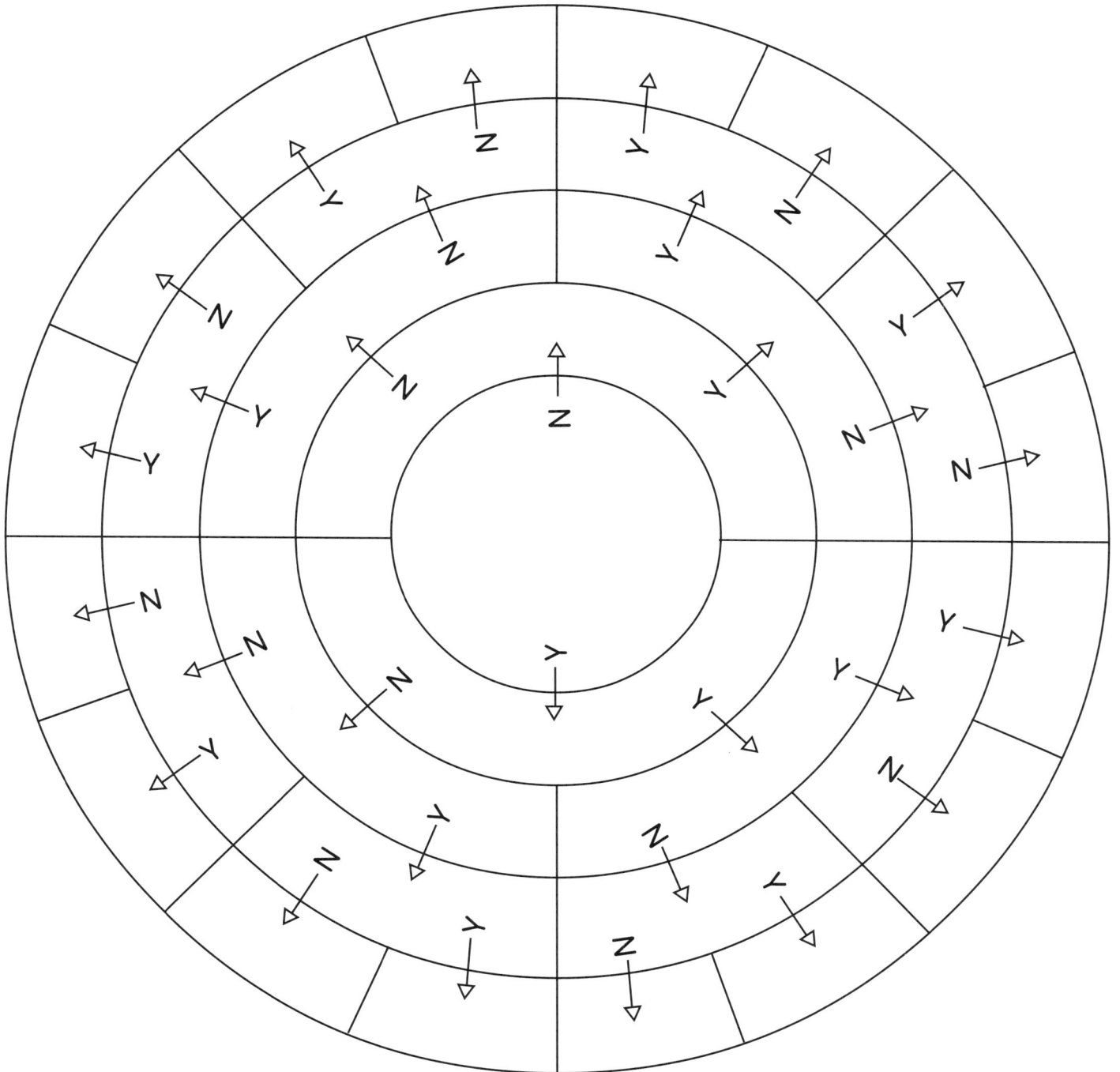

Pupil Sheet 2

● What is your idea about what yeast needs?

_____

_____

_____

_____

● How will you test it? How will you measure it?

_____

_____

_____

_____

● What equipment do you need?

_____

_____

_____

_____

● Are there any risks you need to control?

_____

_____

● How are you going to present the information?

_____

_____

● How will you know if you were right?

_____

_____

_____

_____

Pupil Sheet 3

● These children want to know how to get this dirty water, from a puddle, clean.

We would need to evaporate it

No, that would take too long. We can sieve the bits out

I think the holes in a sieve would be too big to get it really clean

● Who do you agree with?
● When you have decided, tell your teacher.
● Now write a step-by-step description of what the children need to do.

_____

_____

_____

_____

_____

_____

_____

_____

Pupil Sheet 4

● The pure liquid I thought of was _____

It will _____

_____

_____

● The liquid with **undissolved** material in it I thought of was _____

_____ . It will _____

_____

_____

● The liquid with **dissolved** material in it I thought of was _____

_____ . It will _____

_____

_____

● Some useful words:

solution   dissolved
undissolved   evaporates
filter

Pupil Sheet 5

● What is your question about dissolving?

_____

_____

_____

● How will you test it?

_____

_____

_____

_____

_____

_____

● How will you measure?

_____

_____

_____

_____

_____

_____

● What equipment do you need?

_____

_____

_____

_____

● Are there any risks you need to control?

_____

_____

_____

● How are you going to present the information?

_____

_____

_____

_____

_____

_____

Pupil Sheet 6

- Arrange these words to make a concept map.
- When you are satisfied with the arrangement, glue them in place and complete the links.
- If you have any words left over, stick them at the bottom of your sheet.

heating	dissolving
cooling	melting
freezing	evaporating
condensing	burning
change	reversible
irreversible	salt
water	clay
wood	wax
gas	new materials
steam	ice
air	plaster of Paris

Pupil Sheet 7

● Children used identical rubber bands to stretch around pins in clay.

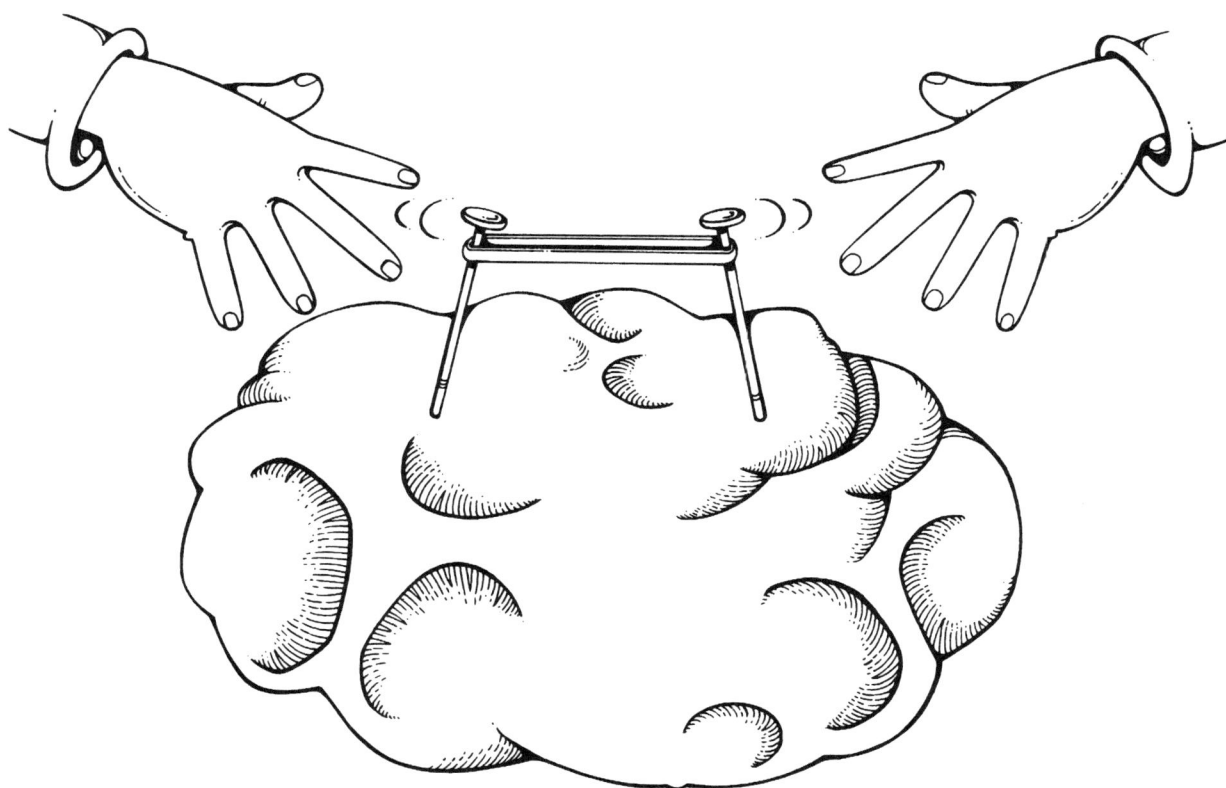

● They changed the distances between the pins.
● This is what happened.

Distance between the pins	Pin position
2cm	upright
4cm	tilted towards one another
6cm	very tilted towards one another
8cm	pulled out of clay

a. Describe what will happen to the pins when they are 3cm apart.

_____

b. Explain why the pins are pulled out when they are 8cm apart.

_____

_____

● Choose one variable that can affect the shadow.

_____

● Prepare a presentation to the others in the class to highlight your question and to show how you would carry out the investigation.

● Draw a table for your results in the space below.

● Convert your data into a line graph using graph paper.

● Write down a question for other children to answer. The question should be about trends, patterns or surprises in the data.

_____

_____

_____

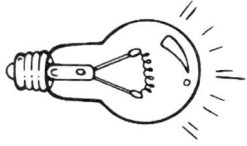

Pupil Sheet 9

- List at least five differences between your wires and write them below.

_____

_____

_____

_____

_____

- Choose one of these variables.
- Predict how changing the wires will affect how well a bulb will light.

_____

_____

_____

_____

_____

- Devise a test to find out if your prediction is right.
- List the equipment you will need to do the test.

_____

_____

_____

_____

_____

_____

- Describe your test.

_____

_____

_____

_____

_____

_____

Pupil Sheet 10

- Children investigated circuits with different lengths of wire and different numbers of batteries (cells).
- They judged how bright the lamps were by seeing how many pieces of tissue paper they could see the light through from the same distance of 1 metre.

- These are their findings.

Circuit description	Layers of tissue paper the lamp can be seen through
4 cells with 1m of wire	3
4 cells with 0.5m of wire	
2 cells with 1m of wire	2
2 cells with 0.5m of wire	4
1 cell with 1m of wire	
1 cell with 0.5m of wire	1

- Using the information in the table complete it with reasonable predictions for:
  4 cells with 0.5cm of wire, 1 cell with 1m of wire.

- Write one or two sentences to summarise these results.

_____

_____

_____

_____

Pupil Sheet 11

- Draw your burglar alarm design here.
- Include a circuit diagram.
- Label the equipment clearly.

- Show your teacher when your design is complete.

- When you are ready, make your design.
- Test it out. Put any modifications you make to improve it on your diagram.
- Make a key to show what the colours mean.

Pupil Sheet 12

● Tell the story of how your burglar alarm developed from your original design to the way it looks now.
● Use each box to draw a picture in and use the space below to write a sentence.

DEVELOPING SCIENTIFIC ENQUIRY – *Year 6*   © Folens (copiable page)

Pupil Sheet 13

- Our question.

_____

_____

_____

- How we are going to collect the best evidence.

_____

_____

_____

_____

_____

_____

_____

_____

_____

_____

- As a group, design your table below.
- Don't forget to think of as many observations as you can, for example, leaf colour and length of leaves as well as your own question.